Six Basic Cooking Techniques

Six Basic Cooking Techniques

CULINARY ESSENTIALS FOR THE HOME COOK

Jennifer Clair

Photographs by Meredith Heuer

HCNY
PRESS

Photographs by Meredith Heuer, www.meredithheuer.com

Book design by Dan Weise, www.thundercut.com

Printed in the United States

HCNY Press
158 Grand Street
New York, NY 10013
www.homecookingny.com

HCNY Press is an imprint of Home Cooking New York LLC.

Publisher's Cataloging-In-Publication Data

Names: Clair, Jennifer. | Heuer, Meredith, photographer.
Title: Six basic cooking techniques : culinary essentials for the home cook / Jennifer Clair ;
    photographs by Meredith Heuer.
Description: New York, NY : HCNY Press, [2018] | Includes index.
Identifiers: ISBN 9780998979205 | ISBN 9780998979212 (ebook)
Subjects: LCSH: Cooking–Technique. | Cooking (Meat) | Cooking (Vegetables) | Sauces. |
    BISAC: COOKING / Methods / General. | COOKING / Methods / Professional. |
    COOKING / Methods / Quick & Easy.
Classification: LCC TX651 .C53 2018 (print) | LCC TX651 (ebook) | DDC 641.5028–dc23

Library of Congress Control Number: 2017915302

For my mother, Phyllis Herman, who prepared home-cooked meals every night of my childhood, with love.

Table of Contents

Making Friends with Your Chef's Knife
Mince, chop, and slice like a pro.

Cooking Meat to Perfection
Make restaurant-quality meals in your own home.

Making Pan Sauces
It's all about the fond.

Roasting Vegetables
Coax out their natural sweetness.

Blanching Green Vegetables
Vivid and crisp-tender every time.

Cooking Leafy Greens
Listen to your mother: "Eat your greens."

Recommended Kitchen Equipment
Having the right tools really makes a difference.

6

Garlicky Broccoli Rabe (with Chickpeas) - pg 72

Recipes to Practice Your Cooking Techniques

8

Fresh Green Herb Sauce (with Hanger Steak) - pg 48

Introduction

You are holding a cookbook that has been informed by thousands of students who have taken this same Six Basic Cooking Techniques class at our school. That school is Home Cooking New York, in downtown Manhattan, where this has been our best-selling class since 2002. So, behold! Our first cookbook — an encapsulation of these six vital techniques sprinkled with the questions and answers that pepper a live class, so you too can benefit from years of our students' queries. Their voice is your voice, and we made sure it is loud and clear throughout the book's chapters, each one highlighting a cooking technique that is instrumental to a solid culinary foundation.

We also made sure the photographs clearly illustrate each technique, as if you were in the classroom with us. The recipes were written with home cooks in mind, so you can practice these six techniques while simultaneously making delicious meals for yourself (and lucky loved ones). The Students Ask and Chefs Say columns in each chapter also grant you inside access to the types of Q&A and kitchen advice that are covered during our cooking classes.

We hope every page of this book answers a culinary question you didn't even know you had. After years of teaching, we've heard them all — and collected them here just for you.

Jennifer Clair

Making Friends with Your Chef's Knife

It is no accident that this is the first chapter of the book. Every home-cooked meal begins with the grip of your chef's knife as you mince, chop, and slice your way to the finish line. So grab hold of the most important tool in your kitchen and let's learn how to get along.

Materials

8-inch chef's knife

Cutting board
(we prefer wood or bamboo)

Handheld 2-stage sharpener

Serrated knife

3½-inch paring knife

Choosing a Chef's Knife

THINGS TO KEEP IN MIND

- A knife is a lifetime investment, so don't be discouraged that a good chef's knife may run you upward of $70. You really only need 3 good knives to cover most kitchen tasks: an 8-inch chef's knife, a 3½-inch paring knife, and a serrated knife (for certain thick-skinned foods like bread, bagels, and tomatoes).

- The best chef's knives are made from hefty high-carbon steel, a strong metal that provides durability and a sharp edge that lasts longer than lower-priced knives made from softer stainless steel. Make sure your knife also has a "full tang," meaning the metal goes through the entire handle. If you can see metal rivets along the handle, or a strip of metal running along the top of the handle, it has a full tang.

- Remember, you only need to buy ONE good chef's knife, so make it count!

BRANDS WE LIKE: Wusthof, Henckels, Mundial

CHEFS SAY

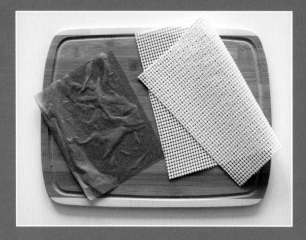

Stabilize your cutting board.

To prevent your board from moving while you are chopping, place it on top of a single, wet paper towel or a reusable rectangle of nonslip drawer liner. A steady board makes for safer knife work.

Steady round food before cutting.

For rounded ingredients (like onions, potatoes, and zucchini), cut a small slice off one side (or just cut in half) so they lie flat on the cutting board for a stable cutting foundation.

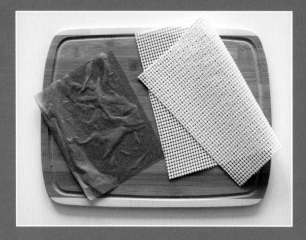

Don't mince basil, mint, or sage.

These delicate herbs turn black (oxidize) with every cut of the knife. To avoid ending up with a pile of blackened herbs, make a chiffonade (see pg 19) instead. This creates thin ribbons of herbs that maintain more of their green color.

Sharpening

It is easier to cut yourself with a dull knife (it doesn't go where you're aiming it), so you need to own one sharpening tool to keep your knife's edge in good shape. (You can also have your knife professionally sharpened at a cookware store; most of them offer this service.) For home cooks, we recommend a handheld 2-stage sharpener. With this, you'll have a well-sharpened knife in a few minutes. **Please note:** This is only for smooth, straight-edged knives; do not use this sharpener on a serrated knife or you will mar its scalloped edge. Also, good sharpening is not easy on the ears; you'll need to endure the jarring sound of grinding metal in order to create a new "edge" on your knife.

1. Hold your knife horizontally and use firm pressure to pull it through the 2 slots (stage I then stage II), from the heel to the tip of the knife, 10 times each.

2. Make sure to press down steadily on the knife during the whole process, so the entire blade is sharpened evenly. The first slot shaves fine metal filings from the knife and the second slot smooths it down for a finished edge.

Holding

Resist the temptation to extend your index finger out over the top of the blade. Rather, use it along with the thumb to pinch each side of the top heel (widest part) of the knife blade, just forward of the handle; this will give you the most control over the blade. The remaining 3 fingers should cradle the underside of the handle.

Slicing Safely

1. ALWAYS hold your knife with the tip safely positioned downward.

2. When slicing, the knife should ALWAYS move in a forward motion, never back toward your body (to avoid jamming the handle into your gut) and never vertically straight up off the cutting board and down, which dulls the blade when it lands on the board.

3. When you are holding something to be cut, ALWAYS curve your fingers to tuck your fingertips under and pop your knuckles out, so the side of the blade rubs against your knuckles, keeping your fingertips safe.

ATTENTION!
THIS IS NOT A KNIFE SHARPENER!
Contrary to a whole lot of popular belief, this long honing steel does not actually sharpen your knife. Instead, it is designed to *straighten* the edge of your knife between sharpenings (over time, a knife's fine edge will bend with normal use). Using the steel can temporarily make your knife seem sharper (further compounding this confusion), but actually your knife is just straighter.

Mincing

1. Place your ingredient in the center of the cutting board. Place the palm of your left hand (or your right, if you are left-handed) on the back of the knife's tip with the fingers extended straight out.

2. Position the ingredient to be minced under the back 3 inches of the knife; this is where the greatest cutting force is exerted, and is the part of the knife that makes solid contact with the cutting board. Do not place food under the front tip of the knife, which pops up when the knife is level on the board.

3. Cut down with a rapid chopping motion. Don't let the front of the blade lose contact with the cutting board; your palm reminds you to keep it down. As the pieces scatter, use the knife's edge (you won't damage it) to gently scrape them back to the center of the board and continue mincing until they are the size you want.

Fresh herbs should be minced until they fall like snow when sprinkled. Garlic should be minced into ¼-inch pieces; mince more finely if using it raw. To mince ginger, first slice it into coins, then finely mince to break down its fibrous material.

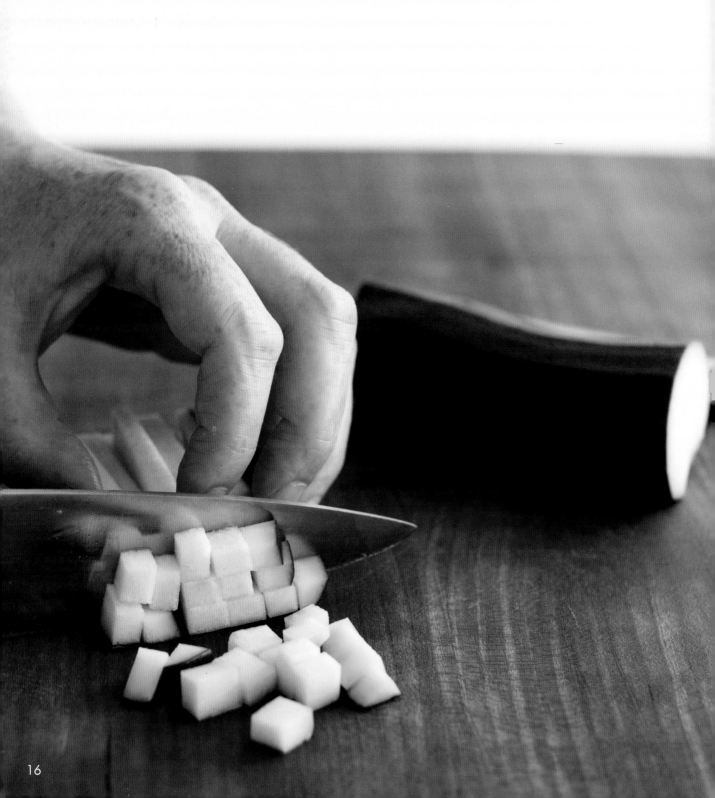

STUDENTS ASK

How often do I sharpen my knife?

The best test is to sharpen your knife right now, then cut something up. Doesn't that feel amazing, how easily it glides through? That is how your knife should always feel. You cannot over sharpen your knife, so sharpening it will never be the wrong decision.

How do I remove the smell of garlic from my hands?

Garlic's potent scent lies in its sticky oils and needs a good scrub with an abrasive, along with hot water and soap, to remove it. Your best bet is rubbing the coarse side of a sponge all over your hands and fingers to remove the fragrant oil. Rubbing your fingers against a stainless-steel utensil under running water or against a cut lemon also does the trick.

How do I keep from crying when cutting an onion?

We have tried it all (putting the onion in the freezer, wearing goggles), but if you are sensitive to onion's sulfuric fumes, your tears are going to flow. Our method for chopping onions is quick and efficient (see pg 18), so crying time is at a minimum. If you are particularly sensitive, makes sure to rinse your cutting board and knife after cutting an onion, so the fumes don't linger.

Cutting an Onion

1. Cut the onion in half from top to bottom, so the root end is still attached to both halves.

2. Place the halves, cut side down, on your board. Cut off the tip of the stem end so you expose a small corner to more easily peel back the papery skin.

3. With the root end away from you, make ¼-inch lengthwise cuts across the onion, leaving about ¼ inch of the onion still attached at the back (root) end; this will hold the onion together as you cut it.

4. Rotate the onion 90° and cut perpendicularly to the lengthwise cuts to make diced onion.

Julienning and Dicing

1. Slice the vegetables lengthwise (you can cut long vegetables — like carrots and zucchini — in half first to make them more manageable).

2. Stack a few slices on top of each other and slice them into matchstick-shaped pieces, the same width as their height, called "julienne."

3. Gather the matchsticks together and slice crosswise into cubes, called "dice."

Making a Chiffonade

This technique is used to cut thin strips of leaves and is primarily used with herbs that need a gentle touch — like basil, mint, and sage — to prevent these oxidizing-prone leaves from turning black.

It is also helpful for cutting large leaves down to size for cooking, like Swiss chard, kale, or collards (see Shredding the Leaves, pg 83).

1. First, stack several leaves on top of each other, with the largest on the bottom.

2. Roll them up crosswise.

3. Thinly slice crosswise from one end of the roll to the other.

CHEFS SAY

Smash your garlic.

To remove the tight, papery skin from a garlic clove, find an object with a flat base (the flat edge of your knife, an olive oil bottle, a can of beans) and gently crush the clove. When the skin splits, you can easily take it off in one piece. Remove the woody base from the clove before mincing.

Peeling ginger is optional.

Really! The thin, papery skin is flavorless and you will never detect it after it is finely minced. You can trim away any particularly rough appendages and dried areas, but otherwise, just wash the ginger before slicing and mincing.

Mise en place!

This is a popular French culinary term, which translates to "put everything in its place." Before you start cooking, have all your ingredients chopped and measured and "in their place," in bowls or arranged on your cutting board. Then you can act like you're on a cooking show, throwing this and that into your pan as you effortlessly cook your dish. This is a cooking game changer.

Don't use pressed garlic for cooking.

The aromatic oils stored inside garlic are sensitive to heat, so pressed garlic will quickly brown in hot oil, marring the sharp, pungent flavor for which it is beloved. Unless you are going to use the garlic raw in a salad dressing or to make gremolata (see pg 76), reach for a chef's knife instead of a garlic press.

Visual Glossary of Knife Cuts

① MINCED PARSLEY

② MINCED GARLIC

③ DICED ONION

④ JULIENNED CARROT

⑤ JULIENNED PEPPER

⑥ DICED PEPPER

⑦ DICED CARROT

⑧ BASIL CHIFFONADE

⑨ SLICED ONION

⑩ ZUCCHINI HALF-MOONS

The Best Vegetable Soup You'll Ever Make

We make this soup during our Knife Skills 101 class, adding each vegetable to the pot as students finish practicing on them. It is a great excuse to practice your own knife skills — consider it a delicious final exam. If you don't feel like chopping 8 different vegetables, you can omit a few. But don't skimp on the anchovies or Parmigiano-Reggiano cheese rind; they are essential to the deep flavor of this soup.

SERVES 8

¼ cup extra-virgin olive oil,
   plus more for drizzling

1 medium onion, diced small

1 fennel bulb, cored and sliced
   very thin

3 cloves garlic, minced

3 anchovy fillets

2 teaspoons minced rosemary

2 large ripe tomatoes, cut into
   1-inch dice

1 red bell pepper, julienned

2 medium carrots, cut into thirds and
   julienned

2 medium potatoes (½ pound), peeled
   and cut into ½-inch dice

1 (14-ounce) can cannellini beans,
   drained but not rinsed

½ cup white wine (optional)

1 (2-ounce) piece Parmigiano-
   Reggiano cheese, rind removed
   and reserved, cheese shaved with
   a vegetable peeler

Kosher salt and a peppermill

1 quart chicken broth, as needed

1 bunch kale, ribs removed and cut into
   1-inch chiffonade

Juice of ½ lemon, as needed

1. In a large, heavy soup pot, heat the oil over medium-high heat. Add the onions and fennel and cook until translucent, about 5 minutes. Add the garlic, anchovies, and rosemary, and cook until the garlic starts to color and the anchovies have begun to dissolve, about 2 minutes. Add the tomatoes, pepper, carrots, potatoes, beans, wine, cheese rind, and 1 teaspoon salt. Add enough broth so the liquid level is 1 inch below the top of the vegetables (you can always add more later).

2. Bring to a boil, then reduce heat to medium-low and simmer, covered, until all the vegetables are tender, at least 25 minutes. Add the kale after 15 minutes of cooking, to preserve its color and texture. Discard the cheese rind and stir in the lemon juice. Season to taste with salt, pepper, and more lemon juice as needed to perk it up.

3. Serve the soup hot or at room temperature with a healthy drizzle of olive oil and a generous handful of Parmigiano-Reggiano shavings.

PARMIGIANO-REGGIANO VS. PARMESAN CHEESE
Parmesan cheese is a hard, salty, aged cow's milk cheese. Parmigiano-Reggiano is the king of this cheese variety; it is made exclusively in Italy and aged for at least 2 years. Its nutty flavor and granular texture are incomparably better than domestic Parmesan, which is aged for less time. Please avoid the non-refrigerated, grated Parmesan sold in supermarkets; it contains a fair amount of non-cheese additives. Look for Parmigiano-Reggiano in the cheese department, with its name stamped on the rind, so you know you're buying the real thing. It is worth making a staple in your refrigerator.

Steak with Classic Red Wine Sauce - pg 42

Cooking Meat to Perfection

A perfectly prepared piece of meat is well within the reach of every home cook. All you need is a little know-how (all included in this chapter) and an instant-read thermometer. The days of poking your steak or slicing it open to see whether it's "done" are over. It's time to cook meat like a chef.

Materials

12-inch stainless steel sauté pan
(with an ovenproof handle)

Tongs

Instant-read thermometer

Cutting board with a well

Ingredients

Meat
(steaks, chops, tenderloins, chicken pieces on the bone)

High-temperature oil
(see pg 31)

Kosher salt and a pepper mill

Preparing

1. **MEAT SHOULD BE DRY AND NOT TOO COLD.**
   Remove the meat from its wrapping and let air-dry, uncovered, on the counter for up to 2 hours; this is the "safe" zone for letting meat sit unrefrigerated, and it is more efficient to cook room-temperature meat. If time is tight, you can skip the de-chilling step and blot dry, if needed, with a paper towel.

2. **SEASON WELL WITH SALT AND PEPPER.**
   "Season high" (sprinkling 8 inches above the meat for an even coating) and only on one side to start. You'll place the meat seasoned side down in the hot pan and then continue seasoning the other side once it is face up in the pan.

Heating the Pan

Heat the pan over medium-high heat, then add the oil to the hot pan (heating the pan first creates a more nonstick surface). To determine when the oil is hot enough to add the meat, tilt the pan and watch the oil. If it moves in thin, fast ripples, it is ready. If the oil is slow and smooth, keep heating. (For meat that is thicker than 1 inch or chicken on the bone, preheat your oven to 375° at this time, because you will need to finish cooking it in the oven.)

Browning

Using tongs, carefully transfer the meat to the hot pan, seasoned side down. Salt and pepper the unseasoned side (now face up). Turn on your exhaust fan, if you have one.

Turning

When the underside of the meat is crisp and deeply browned, 4 to 5 minutes, turn it over. Do not flip the meat over and over, or you will leave too much of its appealing crust on the bottom of the pan. Flip once, and brown the second side.

CHEFS SAY

Make a salt cellar.

You want a one-handed way to add salt to your food when cooking. We recommend a salt cellar, ramekin, or teacup filled with kosher salt, so your fingertips can easily reach in and grab what you need. Keep it out on your counter so everyone knows you mean business in the kitchen.

Please don't wash your chicken.

Holding your chicken under running water greatly increases the risk of cross-contaminating your sink area with droplets of raw chicken juice. We recommend blotting the chicken dry with a paper towel if it is particularly juicy. If you must wash it, make sure your sink is empty of dishes and you thoroughly wipe down the surrounding surfaces afterward. The only way to kill harmful bacteria is to cook the chicken; washing it may only spread it around.

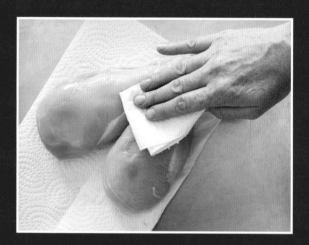

Crisp that chicken skin.

Chicken skin takes longer to crisp up to crackly deliciousness than the bare surface of meat. When cooking chicken with the skin on, give it closer to 8 minutes with the skin side down for the most impressive result.

Cooking Meat More Than 1 Inch Thick

If the meat is thicker than 1 inch — or the chicken is on the bone — additional cooking in the oven is required to cook it through without burning the crispy surface. Preheat the oven to 375° at the same time you start heating your pan, so it is ready when you are finished with the browning step. Make sure your pan has a metal, ovenproof handle; otherwise you'll need to transfer your meat to a baking sheet before putting in the oven. To gauge how much more cooking is needed, check the temperature of the meat before transferring to the oven.

Allow 5 minutes of oven cooking for every 10° to 15° the meat needs to be done.

Checking for Doneness

Use an instant-read thermometer and the chart below to determine when the meat is properly cooked. Use tongs to pick up the meat, then insert the thermometer through the side of the meat so most of the probe is penetrating the meat, avoiding any bones. This will give you the most accurate reading, since you are concerned with the temperature in the center of the meat only.

How to Know When Meat Is Done

STEAK			
125° rare	130° medium rare	140° medium	145° medium well

LAMB CHOPS & DUCK BREAST	PORK CHOPS & TENDERLOIN	CHICKEN	
130° medium rare	145° medium well	160° breasts	165° thighs & legs

Resting

Once the meat is perfectly cooked, let it rest for 5 minutes before slicing. The meat needs this time to redistribute juices to its extremities, which have contracted during cooking. A rest allows more of the juices to stay in the meat during slicing, as opposed to rushing out onto your cutting board. If you are not eating promptly after the 5-minute resting period, tent the meat loosely with foil; the temperature will hold for about 15 minutes.

Slicing Meat

Some meats have a grain, or a distinct direction of the meat's fibers, and it will determine which direction you will slice it for serving. Flank, hanger, and skirt steaks — and chicken breast — all have grains. Before slicing these meats, determine the direction of the grain by gently pulling the meat apart to see the direction of the fibers. Hold your knife perpendicular to the direction of the fibers and slice into ½-inch pieces to achieve the most tender cut of meat. If there is no grain, slice it in any direction you like.

KOSHER SALT   SEA SALT   FLAKY SEA SALT

Cooking with Salt

We recommend cooking with **kosher salt** for its coarse texture. It is perfect for pinching and sprinkling over food, because you can feel it and see it easily. We don't recommend table salt for use in the kitchen; it is hard to hold in your fingertips, dissolves too quickly to see where you've sprinkled it, and leaves behind the trace metallic tang of iodine (most table salt is iodized). **Sea salt** is great for seasoning a dish just before serving (especially salads and sliced meats) so you can enjoy the clean, briny crunch for which sea salt is prized. Our favorite is **flaky sea salt**; the soft white crystals can easily be crushed with your fingertips over a finished dish.

Understanding High-Heat Oils

Nature's unprocessed oils and fats (like extra-virgin olive oil and butter) can't withstand the high heat needed to properly sear steak, deep fry, or cook in a wok, so you need to stock a good-quality high-heat oil. Since most high-heat oils are processed and refined (required to remove every natural particle that might burn), your best choice is to buy a "neutral" oil (meaning flavorless) like avocado, grapeseed, or safflower oil that is:

1. **SOLD IN A GLASS BOTTLE**
   (no leaching of plastic chemicals)

2. **EXPELLER PRESSED OR COLD PRESSED**
   (extracted by pressing as opposed to chemical solvents)

3. **ORGANIC**
   (ensuring that it is not derived from a GMO, genetically modified organism)

Please note: When sautéing and roasting vegetables, and browning small pieces of meat, it is fine to use unprocessed fats and oils. See Enjoy the Good Fats, pg 40.

STUDENTS ASK

Should I cover my pan to reduce splatter?

No. When you cover your pan, water vapor collects under the lid and falls back onto your food, steaming it instead of browning it. Instead, use a splatter screen, an immensely handy kitchen tool that traps cooking splatter and protects your arms and stovetop from hot spits of oil. The screen allows steam from the cooking meat to pass through so it does not hinder the browning process.

Can I use a nonstick pan?

This question is asked once every class. And we understand; no one likes scrubbing. But we don't recommend nonstick cookware for cooking anything but eggs, potatoes, and pancakes. Everything else benefits from the beautiful caramelization that happens when food browns onto the bottom of a pan, especially meat. A little liquid will always remove (deglaze) browned-on bits from the bottom of a pan. Check out The Clean Pan Club (pg 41).

When should I use my convection oven?

If you have this setting on your oven, use it every time you cook. This setting activates a small fan built into the back of the oven, circulating the air during cooking. This results in better browning and a more efficient cooking time. If using convection, shave off 10 minutes for every hour of cooking time, making sure to check your food accordingly. For baking, lower the oven temperature by 25° because ingredients like butter and sugar brown more quickly than meats and vegetables.

Pan-Roasted Chicken with Sherry-Thyme Gravy • pg 43

Making Pan Sauces

It's all about the fond. Fond, the browned-on meaty juices that stick to the bottom of your pan after you've cooked a piece of meat, is the beginning of every good pan sauce. There are two kinds of pan sauces: reduction sauces and thickened sauces (gravies). They vary in texture and intensity, and both allow you to harness the flavor left behind in the pan and return it to where it rightfully belongs: on your food.

Materials

Fond-covered pan
(caramelized crust left behind after cooking meat)

Liquid measuring cup

Flat-edged wooden utensil, for scraping up fond

Ingredients

Wine

Chicken broth

Herbs
(thyme, rosemary, bay leaf)

Unsalted butter
(only for reductions)

All-purpose flour
(only for gravies)

Kosher salt and a pepper mill

Making a Reduction Sauce

This is the quickest and easiest of the pan sauces. Liquid is added to the same pan you used to cook meat — which is now crusted with caramelized meat juices, called fond — and boiled down (reduced) to create a concentrated and fully flavored sauce.

DEGLAZING

With your pan over medium-high heat, add the sauce liquids (see pg 39) to the hot pan. The liquid will begin to work its magic on the fond immediately, loosening and liquefying it, hence the term "deglazing." Using a flat-edged utensil, gently clean the fond off the bottom of the pan so it can be incorporated into the sauce.

REDUCING

Allow the liquid to reduce by half, about 4 minutes. Boiling off half the water content concentrates the sauce's flavor.

FINISHING

Remove your pan from the heat (very important!) and add unsalted butter to the pan. Allow it to melt, swirling the pan to fully incorporate the butter into the sauce. **Please note:** It is crucial to remove the pan from the heat before adding the butter. If the sauce is simmering, the butter will "break" out of its emulsified state, creating an oily sauce instead of the desired creamy one.

Making a Gravy

Gravy is a pan sauce distinguished by the addition of a roux (a mixture of fat and flour), which thickens the sauce to a consistency that is beloved for blanketing everything from pork chops to your Thanksgiving mashed potatoes. Use the same pan you cooked your meat in to build your gravy.

MAKING A ROUX

You need a fat-to-flour ratio of 1:1 to make a proper roux. If you have fat left over in the pan from cooking meat, that is ideal. If not, you must add more fat to your fond-covered pan (butter or olive oil will do). With your pan over medium heat, sprinkle the flour onto the hot fat and stir until the fat has absorbed all the flour, about 1 minute.

DEGLAZING

Add the sauce liquids to the hot pan. The liquid will begin to work its magic on the fond immediately, loosening and liquefying it, hence the term "deglazing." Using a flat-edged utensil, gently clean the fond off the bottom of the pan so it can be incorporated into the sauce. **Please note:** If you are using wine, add it to the hot pan first and allow it to cook for 1 minute before adding any additional liquid. This boils off the alcohol and caramelizes the wine's fruity flavors.

THICKENING

When the gravy comes to a boil, the starch in the flour swells up and thickens the sauce. Once it thickens, continue cooking to develop the flavor, stirring frequently, about 2 minutes more.

SEASONING

Start tasting! The gravy will likely need some salt (especially if you used unsalted broth). A good gravy should make you smile when you taste it.

STUDENTS ASK

What kind of wine should I use for cooking?

The answer is simple: Cook with wine you like to drink; no one varietal will make or break a dish. That doesn't mean your finest bottle, but it should be palatable and not "cooking wine" from the supermarket, which has added salt and preservatives and is literally undrinkable. Single-serving wine bottles from a wine shop are a great pantry staple, so you don't have to open a whole bottle when the recipe call for a small amount.

What can I substitute for wine in a pan sauce?

If you are not inclined to use alcohol, you can substitute ¾ teaspoon of vinegar (red wine, white wine, sherry, apple cider, or rice) or lemon juice for ⅓ cup of wine (do not attempt this substitution if the sauce calls for more than ⅓ cup of wine). Taste, adding ¼ teaspoon more at a time until the sauce tastes bright.

How do I choose the best meat?

Several important keywords can help you choose the best quality of meat. When possible, buy your meat from a butcher (in-store butchers are fine), so you can ask all the questions you need to about its quality. For chicken and pork, the most important descriptors are "pasture raised," "organic," "antibiotic free," and "humanely raised." For beef, "grass fed" is the golden rule, along with the previous keywords. "Organic" labeling means the animal was never fed antibiotics, which is always a good thing.

Flavorful Liquids = Delicious Sauces

Try these combos to make either a reduction sauce or a gravy. For these liquid quantities, a reduction sauce needs 1 tablespoon of unsalted butter swirled in at the end (off the heat), and a gravy needs to start with a roux (1 tablespoon of flour added to 1 tablespoon of hot fat). See pgs 36–37 for step-by-step instructions.

For pork chops or tenderloin	For chicken or turkey	For steak (reduction only)
½ cup apple cider	1 cup chicken broth	1 cup red wine
1 cup chicken broth	⅓ cup white wine or dry sherry	⅓ cup chicken broth
1 sprig rosemary		1 sprig thyme or bay leaf
1 tablespoon red wine vinegar or cider vinegar	1 sprig rosemary or thyme	

Enjoy the Good Fats

Fat is a vital component of good-tasting food and a balanced, healthy diet. But all fats are not equal, so it is important to choose the "good fats" when stocking your own kitchen. Cooking at home affords you the only chance to choose the quality of fat you consume, since the types of cooking fats used in restaurants, take-out joints, and prepackaged meals are generally of poor quality (mass food production errs on the side of economics when sourcing ingredients). So what are the "good fats"? They are natural and unprocessed fats, their flavor and nutrition unadulterated by chemicals, technology, or refinement.

GOOD FATS ARE FULL OF FLAVOR:

1. BUTTER

2. EXTRA-VIRGIN OLIVE OIL

3. ANY KIND OF RENDERED ANIMAL FAT
(bacon, chicken, duck, but not the hydrogenated lard from the supermarket)

4. EXTRA-VIRGIN COCONUT OIL

5. ALL TOASTED NUT AND SEED OILS
(sesame, walnut, hazelnut, pumpkin seed, flax; all best used uncooked)

If you need a "neutral" (flavorless) oil for high-heat cooking like deep frying or wok cooking, or for some baked goods, consult the guidelines for buying those on pg 31.

THE CLEAN PAN CLUB

The best part of making a pan sauce is how beautifully it cleans your crusty pan! No scrubbing for you; just a pint of delicious gravy.

Steak with Classic Red Wine Sauce

This is the best way to enjoy a good steak. The acidic red wine reduction is softened by a swirl of sweet butter at the end, making it the ultimate complement to steak's rich flavor. Any drinkable red wine will do, but a full-bodied, fruity red will yield the deepest flavor: Cabernet, Merlot, or Pinot Noir. If your steaks are thicker than 1 inch, make sure to preheat the oven to 375° before heating the pan. Thick steaks need additional cooking time in the oven after the browning step to ensure that they are properly cooked through.

SERVES 4

1 tablespoon high-heat oil
  (see pg 31)

2 pounds hanger, rib-eye, or sirloin
  steak (or your favorite cut), 1 inch
  thick

Kosher salt and a pepper mill

1 cup red wine

⅓ cup chicken broth

1 sprig thyme or 1 bay leaf

1 tablespoon unsalted butter

1. Heat the oil in a large sauté pan over medium-high heat. Season the steaks with salt and pepper on one side only. When the oil is hot enough to ripple, add the steaks, seasoned side down. Season the other side with salt and pepper. Cook until they are deeply browned and register 130° on an instant-read thermometer, about 5 minutes per side for medium rare (or to your desired temperature; see When Meat Is Done, pg 29). Transfer the steaks to a cutting board with a well and let rest for 5 minutes.

2. Meanwhile, make the pan sauce: To the hot pan, add the wine, broth, and thyme, scraping the browned-on bits (fond) off the bottom of the pan to incorporate it into the sauce. Bring to a boil, then reduce heat to medium and simmer until the sauce is reduced by half, about 5 minutes.

3. Remove the pan from the heat and add the butter. **Please note:** If not removed from the heat, the butter will melt too quickly and "break," turning the sauce oily. Swirl the pan until the butter is completely incorporated. Remove the thyme.

4. Slice the steaks ½ inch thick and serve with the red wine sauce poured over the top.

Pan-Roasted Chicken with Sherry-Thyme Gravy

This is a classic roast chicken and gravy recipe, despite the fancified "sherry-thyme" addition. But sherry and thyme are the keys to making a gravy that knocks your socks off. You can even use this same gravy recipe for your next Thanksgiving bird. Best of all, sherry is a fortified wine (meaning brandy is added to it), so it keeps almost forever on the shelf, ensuring that you always have it on hand.

SERVES 4

8 chicken thighs or 4 chicken breasts,
  skin on, bone in

Kosher salt and a pepper mill

1 tablespoon extra-virgin olive oil,
    plus more as needed

2 tablespoons all-purpose flour

⅓ cup dry sherry or white wine

1½ cups chicken broth

1 sprig thyme

1. Preheat the oven to 375°. Season the chicken with salt and pepper on the skin side only.

2. Heat 1 tablespoon of the oil in a large sauté pan over medium-high heat. When the oil is hot enough to ripple, add the chicken pieces, skin side down, and cook until the skin is a deep golden brown, about 8 minutes. Wait until the skin easily pulls away from the bottom of the pan (if it sticks, the chicken is not ready to be turned; continue cooking for another 2 minutes). Turn the chicken over and transfer the pan to the oven.

3. Cook until the chicken registers 160° for breasts and 165° for thighs on an instant-read thermometer, about 20 to 25 minutes for thick breasts, and 15 to 20 minutes for thighs. Transfer the chicken to a serving plate.

4. Make the gravy: Immediately wrap the handle of the hot pan in a potholder or kitchen towel (to remind you that it's hot) and transfer to the stovetop over medium-high heat.

5. If there is less than 2 tablespoons of chicken fat in the pan, add enough olive oil to make 2 tablespoons of fat. Sprinkle the flour over the sizzling fat and cook, stirring, until the chalky flour disappears (is absorbed by the oil). Add the sherry to the hot pan and cook for 1 minute, scraping the browned-on bits (fond) off the bottom of the pan to incorporate it into the gravy. Add the broth and thyme and bring to a boil. Cook for 2 minutes, stirring, until thickened. Season to taste with salt. Pour the sauce over the chicken, and serve immediately.

Pan-Roasted Lemon-Rosemary Chicken

This is our most requested recipe, and you are about to see why. The chicken and sauce are juicy and flavorful, and the dish is efficient, to boot: While the chicken skin is crisping in the pan, you are squeezing lemons and mincing garlic and rosemary. Please don't be tempted to use bottled lemon juice for this recipe; you really need that citrus zing only found in fresh lemons.

SERVES 4

8 chicken thighs or 4 chicken breasts,
  skin on, bone in
Kosher salt and a pepper mill
3 tablespoons extra-virgin olive oil
Juice of 2 lemons (about ⅓ cup)
3 cloves garlic, minced
1 tablespoon minced rosemary

1. Preheat the oven to 375°. Season the chicken with salt and pepper on the skin side only.

2. Heat 1 tablespoon of the oil in a large sauté pan over medium-high heat. When the oil is hot enough to ripple, add the chicken pieces skin side down and cook until the skin is a deep golden brown, about 8 minutes. Wait until the skin easily pulls away from the bottom of the pan (if it sticks, the chicken is not ready to be turned; continue cooking for another 2 minutes).

3. Meanwhile, make the lemon sauce: In a small bowl, combine the lemon juice, remaining 2 tablespoons olive oil, the garlic, rosemary, and ½ teaspoon salt. Set aside.

4. Turn the chicken so the crisp skin is face up. Pour the sauce over the chicken and scrape up the browned-on bits (fond) off the bottom of the pan to incorporate into the lemon sauce. Transfer the whole pan to the oven and cook until the chicken registers 160° for breasts and 165° for thighs on an instant-read thermometer, about 20 to 25 minutes for thick breasts and 15 to 20 minutes for thighs.

5. Serve the chicken with the lemony pan sauce spooned over the top.

Chicken Piccata with Capers and Caramelized Lemons

Bright with salty capers, caramelly lemon slices, and good old butter, this piccata sauce is good enough to drink from a spoon and gives pizazz to chicken breast's mild flavor. The flour that dusts the chicken helps build up the brown crust on the bottom of the pan, creating a sauce with a real depth of flavor and a velvety texture.

SERVES 4

2 tablespoons extra-virgin olive oil

1½ pounds boneless skinless chicken breasts, each sliced in half horizontally, to make thinner breasts

Kosher salt and a pepper mill

½ cup all-purpose flour, on a plate

2 tablespoons unsalted butter

1 washed and unpeeled lemon, thinly sliced and seeded

2 cloves garlic, minced

¼ cup capers

½ cup white wine

¾ cup chicken broth

2 tablespoons minced fresh parsley, for garnish (optional)

1. In a large sauté pan, heat the oil over medium-high heat. Season the chicken with salt and pepper on both sides, then lightly dredge the chicken breast halves in the flour, patting firmly to remove all but the thinnest coating of flour.

2. Add the flour-dusted chicken to the pan, in batches, and cook until it is golden brown on both sides and registers 160° on an instant-read thermometer, 4 to 5 minutes per side depending on the thickness of the chicken. When done, transfer the chicken to a plate and repeat until all the chicken is cooked.

3. To the hot pan, add 1 tablespoon of the butter. Add the lemon slices and cook until golden brown on each side. Add the garlic and cook for 1 minute, stirring. Add the capers and wine and cook for 1 minute, scraping up the browned-on bits (fond) off the bottom of the pan. Add the broth and bring to a boil and cook until the sauce is reduced by half and is well thickened, about 4 minutes.

4. Remove the pan from the heat and add the remaining tablespoon butter. **Please note:** If not removed from the heat, the butter will melt too quickly and "break," turning the sauce oily. Swirl the pan until the butter is completely incorporated. Return the chicken to the pan to warm through. Serve, garnished with the parsley, if desired.

Pork Tenderloin with Bacon–Apple Cider Gravy

Pork tenderloin, bacon, apples. These are reason enough to make this recipe. You really can't improve upon this trifecta of goodness.

SERVES 4

4 strips bacon

2 pork tenderloins (about 2 pounds total)

Kosher salt and a pepper mill

1 small onion, sliced thin

1 crisp apple (Gala, Empire, Fuji), skin on, cored, and sliced thin

2 tablespoons all-purpose flour

⅔ cup apple cider (nonalcoholic) or apple juice

1⅓ cups chicken broth

2 teaspoons apple cider vinegar or red wine vinegar

1 sprig thyme or rosemary

1. Add the bacon to a large sauté pan over medium high heat. Cook until it renders its fat and crisps, about 8 minutes, turning as needed. Transfer the bacon to a paper towel–lined plate and pour off (and save) all but 2 tablespoons of the fat from the pan.

2. Season the tenderloins with salt and pepper on one side only and add them to the hot pan, seasoned side down. Season the other side with salt and pepper. Cook until browned on both sides, about 8 minutes total. Transfer the tenderloins to another plate.

3. Make the gravy: Add 2 tablespoons of the reserved bacon fat to the pan and add the onion, apple, and a generous sprinkle of salt, cooking until the apples are lightly browned, about 5 minutes. Sprinkle the flour over the apples and cook, stirring, until the flour disappears (is absorbed by the oil). Add the cider, broth, vinegar, and thyme. Bring to a boil, scraping the browned-on bits (fond) off the bottom of the pan to incorporate it into the gravy.

4. Return the tenderloins to the pan along with any accumulated juices. Return to a boil, reduce heat to medium-low, cover, and cook until the pork registers 145° on an instant-read thermometer, 6 to 10 minutes, depending on the thickness of the tenderloin.

5. Transfer the pork to a cutting board with a well and let rest for 5 minutes. Remove the thyme sprig and taste the gravy, seasoning it with salt and more vinegar, as needed, to make it taste bright.

6. Slice the tenderloin 1 inch thick and serve with the rich gravy and crumbled reserved bacon on top (and don't fret if your bacon mysteriously disappears before the dish is finished: cook's treat).

Pork Chops with Grape-Rosemary Reduction

Pork plus fruit is a winning combination. Red grapes are a year-round supermarket staple, and this pan sauce is also terrific using other red fruits, especially pitted cherries (fresh or frozen) or sliced plums. Pork is bred to be very lean nowadays, so make sure to catch these chops at 145° or they will lose too much of their precious juices.

SERVES 4

2 tablespoons bacon fat or extra-virgin olive oil

4 rib or loin pork chops, 1 inch thick (about 2 pounds)

Kosher salt and a pepper mill

1 cup halved seedless red grapes, pitted fresh or frozen cherries, or 1 plum, pitted and sliced thin

½ cup chicken broth

¼ cup port, sherry, or red wine

1 tablespoon red wine vinegar or balsamic vinegar

1 sprig rosemary

1. Heat the fat or oil in a large sauté pan over medium-high heat. Season the pork chops with salt and pepper on one side only. When the oil is hot enough to ripple, add the chops, seasoned side down. Season the other side with salt and pepper. Cook until the pork is well browned and registers 145° on an instant-read thermometer, 4 to 5 minutes per side. Transfer the chops to a serving plate and let rest for 5 minutes.

2. Meanwhile, make the pan sauce: To the hot pan still over medium-high heat, add the grapes, broth, port, vinegar, and rosemary, and cook until reduced by half, about 5 minutes. Remove from heat and discard the rosemary. Season to taste with salt, as needed.

3. Serve the pork chops with the pan sauce poured over the top.

Fresh Green Herb Sauce

This is not a pan sauce! However, we included it in the book simply because we bow down to this fresh and fully flavored sauce, and it needed to be included in our first book. It is excellent as an accompaniment to all browned meats (steak, chicken, pork, even lamb) and all manner of fish, and as a dip for roasted and blanched vegetables. It's also good with your morning eggs and as a sandwich spread. You can substitute cilantro for half of the parsley for a more diverse flavor.

MAKES ABOUT 1 CUP

⅓ cup slivered or sliced almonds (toasted in a dry skillet until golden; this step is optional)

1 large clove garlic

½ teaspoon kosher salt

Juice of ½ lemon (2 tablespoons)

2 cups packed flat-leaf parsley leaves

2 anchovy fillets

2 tablespoons capers

½ cup extra-virgin olive oil

In the bowl of a food processor, combine the nuts, garlic, and salt until very finely ground. Add the lemon juice, parsley, anchovies, and capers and purée until roughly chopped. With the machine running, drizzle in the oil until it makes a smooth sauce, scraping down the sides of the processor with a rubber spatula. Serve at room temperature. Can be stored in the refrigerator for up to 5 days.

Fluffy Mashed Potatoes

Because every good pan sauce deserves a bed of light and fluffy mashed potatoes, we made sure to include this foolproof recipe. The key is to reserve at least 1 cup of the potato cooking water before draining. Using this liquid in place of traditional milk or cream protects the delicate flavor of the potatoes from being overwhelmed by the heavy taste of hot dairy. Also, always use a potato masher or ricer to mash potatoes, never anything with a blade or a paddle; cutting or beating cooked potatoes releases excess starch and gives the potatoes a gluey texture.

SERVES 4

2 pounds russet baking potatoes, peeled and cut into 2-inch pieces

Kosher salt and a pepper mill

4 tablespoons unsalted butter (do not skimp!)

1. Place the potatoes and 2 teaspoons salt in a large pot and add enough water to cover the potatoes by 1 inch. Place the pot over medium-high heat and bring to a boil. Reduce heat to medium-low, cover, and simmer until the potatoes are very tender when pierced with a fork, 15 to 20 minutes.

2. Using a Pyrex measuring cup, remove and reserve 1 cup of the potato cooking water. Drain the potatoes into a colander set in the sink and immediately return them to the hot empty pot.

3. Add all of the butter and ⅓ cup of the potato water to start. Mash until the potatoes are smooth and the butter is well incorporated. Add more cooking water as needed to make creamy potatoes. Add more salt and pepper to taste, starting with at least ½ teaspoon of salt and 5 good grinds of black pepper. Mashed potatoes need aggressive seasoning to be their best. Serve warm.

Rosemary-Roasted Butternut Squash, Potatoes, and Red Onions - pg 58

Roasting Vegetables

This is — hands down — the easiest and most rewarding way to cook vegetables. Five minutes of prep time and then it's 100% unattended cooking, freeing you up to prepare the rest of your meal. Let the oven work its magic, creating tender vegetables tinged with a natural caramelized sweetness.

Materials

Rimmed baking sheet
Large mixing bowl
Mixing spoon
Thin spatula

GOOD VEGETABLES TO ROAST

butternut squash
potatoes
sweet potatoes
carrots
eggplant
zucchini
mushrooms
peppers
Brussels sprouts
fennel
onions
cauliflower
cherry tomatoes

Ingredients

Just about any vegetable
Extra-virgin olive oil
Kosher salt and a pepper mill

Vegetable Size

Bite sized
You shouldn't need a knife to eat them.

Uniformity
When it comes to roasting, it's a golden rule. Everything will be evenly browned and tender.

Vegetable Combinations

Many "like" vegetables can be roasted together on the same baking sheet because they cook at the same rate.

"Unlike" vegetables can be cooked at the same time, just on separate baking sheets, because their cooking times will vary.

ROOT VEGETABLES	CRUNCHY VEGETABLES	SOFT VEGETABLES
carrots	peppers	eggplant
potatoes	fennel	zucchini
sweet potatoes	asparagus	mushrooms
butternut squash*	broccoli	cherry tomatoes
parsnips	cabbage	
onions	Brussels sprouts	
beets	cauliflower	

*Technically not a root vegetable, but it has a similar texture.

Seasoning

Add olive oil, salt, pepper, and optional seasonings to vegetables in a large mixing bowl, then toss well to coat. Transfer to a baking sheet.

Arranging

Take care to arrange vegetables, cut side down (if they have a cut side), in a single layer on your baking sheet, so they all have a chance to brown against the hot metal.

Roasting

In a 375° oven, roast until golden brown on the underside. Do not be tempted to stir the vegetables as they roast; you will disturb their developing crust. Start checking for browning and tenderness after 30 minutes of roasting. Cooking time for each type of vegetable will vary, but 30 minutes is a great benchmark to start peeking in the oven.

Resting

Let the vegetables rest for 5 minutes on the baking sheet before trying to remove them with the spatula. For starchier vegetables (potatoes!), this quick resting period allows them to naturally steam themselves off the hot sheet so you don't leave any golden crust behind.

Removing

A thin, hard spatula (metal or plastic) is your best friend here to remove the vegetables from the baking sheet intact.

Flavor Combinations

SAVORY

EGGPLANT
ZUCCHINI
FENNEL
PEPPERS
TOMATOES
MUSHROOMS
ONIONS

with
Coriander
Cumin
Sumac
Za'atar
Oregano
Rosemary
Parsley
Thyme

SWEET

SWEET POTATOES
CARROTS
WINTER SQUASH

with
Smoked paprika
Cumin
Curry powder
Garam masala
Rosemary
Sage

MILD

CAULIFLOWER
POTATOES

with
Everything
(Really, they play well with any of the spices and herbs listed here.)

A few favorites: **sumac** *(deep red spice with a lemony tang),* **za'atar** *(Middle Eastern spice mix of dried thyme, sumac, and sesame seeds),* **smoked paprika** *(richly fragrant spice that adds a deep smokiness and charred warmth to food), and* **garam masala** *(warm Indian spice blend).*

STUDENTS ASK

What is "extra-virgin" olive oil?

This is the gold standard for olive oil. "Extra-virgin" means the oil is extracted from the first pressing of the olives (subsequent pressings create less flavorful, less nutrient-dense oil) and the olives are cold pressed (without heat or chemicals). This oil has the maximum amount of flavor, antioxidants, and vitamins still intact; heat destroys many of these qualities. There is no reason to use anything but extra-virgin when choosing a cooking oil (for exceptions, see pg 31); your food deserves the best quality of oil.

Should I line my pan with foil?

No. If you let your roasted vegetables rest before removing them from the pan (at least 5 minutes), they will easily slide off, leaving no hardened crust behind. Cherry tomatoes are the one exception; during roasting, their juicy insides leak out and form a sticky crust. All other vegetables brown better in direct contact with the hot metal of the pan. If you must line your pan, we prefer parchment paper over foil (no metallic taste or waste!).

How long do spices last?

Ground spices generally lose their flavor after a year or two. To determine whether your spices are up to snuff, give them a sniff. If they have a strong aroma, they're fine. If they smell like dust, then dump them in the trashcan. Three factors diminish a spice's potency: time, light, and heat. You can't stop time, but you can store your spices away from light and heat in an overhead cabinet, far from the stove, to prolong their culinary usefulness.

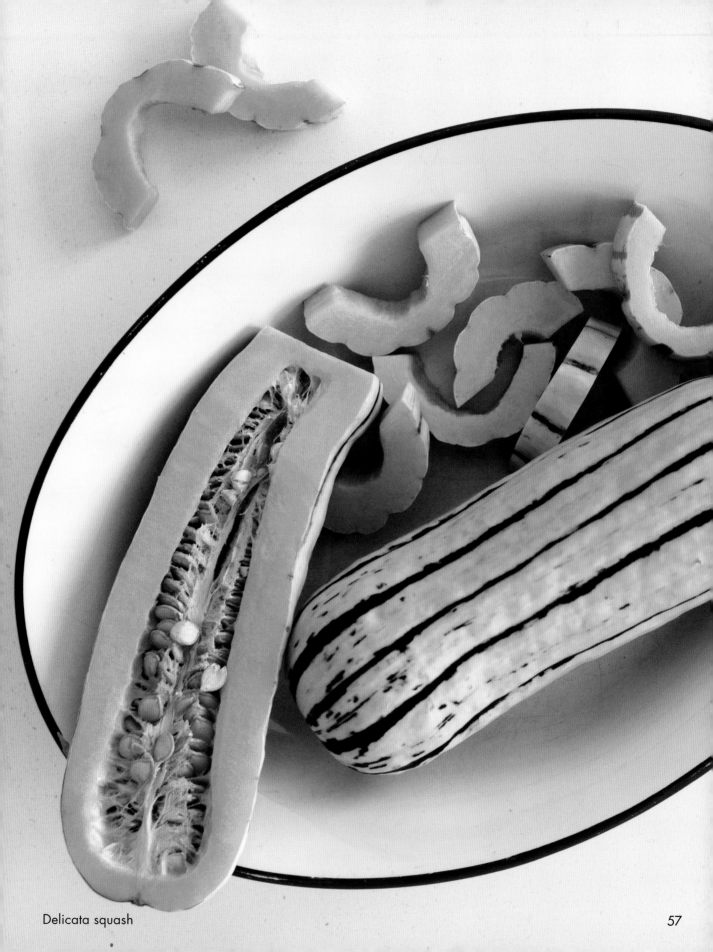

Delicata squash

Rosemary-Roasted Potatoes, Butternut Squash, and Red Onion

For the best roasted potatoes, choose the smallest ones you can find; the more times you have to cut them, the more places they lose moisture while roasting. An ideal potato should only need to be cut in half once to be bite sized. This way the cut side can brown against the hot metal of the baking sheet and the flesh can steam to creaminess inside its protective skin.

SERVES 4

1 pound small potatoes (fingerling, red, new, or purple), cut in half lengthwise

1 large red onion, peeled and cut into ½-inch-thick wedges, with some of the root attached at the base to hold the layers together

1 small butternut squash (1 pound), peeled, seeded, and cut into 1-inch cubes

¼ cup extra-virgin olive oil

1 tablespoon minced rosemary, thyme, or sage

Kosher salt and a pepper mill

1. Preheat the oven to 375°. In a large mixing bowl, combine the potatoes, onion wedges, butternut squash, oil, the herbs, 1 teaspoon salt, and a few grindings of pepper; toss until the vegetables are evenly coated. Transfer to a rimmed baking sheet and arrange all the vegetables cut side down.

2. Roast until the vegetables are tender and the underside is golden brown, about 40 minutes. Let the vegetables rest for 5 minutes on the baking sheet before removing with a thin spatula. This gives them a chance to steam themselves off the pan's surface, so you don't leave any of their sweet crust behind.

3. Serve warm or at room temperature.

Curry-Roasted Delicata Squash

Delicata (see photo, pg 57) are beautiful, oblong winter squash that appear in the markets in the fall. They are all the more special because they only show up seasonally (whereas you can find acorn and butternut squash year-round). They have a bright orange flesh and green-and-orange-striped skin; the sweetest ones have more orange than green. Best of all, their skin is edible, so no peeling is required! The roasted skin offers a perfect counterpoint to the buttery soft flesh. Smoked paprika is another great spice pairing with delicata; just substitute it for the curry in this recipe when you want a smoky treat.

SERVES 4

2 large delicata squash, cut in half lengthwise and seeded

3 tablespoons extra-virgin olive oil

Kosher salt and a pepper mill

2 teaspoons curry powder

1. Preheat the oven to 375°. Cut the squash into ½-inch half-moons.

2. In a large mixing bowl, toss the squash with the oil, 1 teaspoon salt, a few grindings of pepper, and the curry powder. Transfer to a rimmed baking sheet and spread out in a single layer for even browning.

3. Roast until the squash is tender and the undersides are golden brown, about 30 minutes. Let the squash rest for 5 minutes on the baking sheet before removing with a thin spatula. This gives them a chance to steam themselves off the pan's surface, so you don't leave any of their sweet crust behind.

4. Serve warm or at room temperature. This squash is also delicious eaten cold straight from the fridge, as a snack.

Smoky Sweet Potato Fries

Smoked paprika and sweet potatoes are a dream duo, and these smoky, sweet, and salty oven-roasted fries are quite addictive. Preheating the baking sheet for this recipe ensures fries with a deep golden crust.

SERVES 4

4 sweet potatoes (about 2 pounds), scrubbed

¼ cup extra-virgin olive oil

1 tablespoon smoked paprika

Kosher salt

1. Preheat the oven to 400°. Place a rimmed baking sheet in the oven while it is preheating.

2. Slice the potatoes lengthwise (with or without the skin) into ½-inch slices, and cut again into ½-inch julienne (french fry shape). Place the potatoes in a bowl and toss with the olive oil, paprika, and ½ teaspoon salt.

3. Using a potholder, remove the hot baking sheet from the oven and arrange the potatoes (carefully) in a single layer. Roast until the potatoes are golden brown on the bottom and tender, about 40 minutes. Let the potatoes rest for 5 minutes on the baking sheet before removing with a thin spatula. This gives them a chance to steam themselves off the pan's surface, so you don't leave any of their sweet crust behind.

4. Sprinkle with additional salt as needed. Serve hot.

Roasted Ratatouille with Olives and Basil

Ratatouille is a deeply satisfying Southern French dish made by individually cooking 5 different vegetables to perfection. While this creates unbeatable flavor, it also poses a lengthy task for the home cook. This recipe simplifies the steps needed to make a classic ratatouille without sacrificing flavor. The eggplant and zucchini roast and caramelize in the oven while you cook the juicier vegetables together to make a rich base. The addition of briny olives and fresh basil at the end further brighten this traditional dish.

SERVES 6

1 large eggplant, cut into 1-inch cubes

6 tablespoons extra-virgin olive oil

Kosher salt and a pepper mill

2 large zucchini (about 1 pound),
  cut into 1-inch half-moons

1 medium onion, diced

2 orange or yellow bell peppers,
  cut into 1-inch squares

½ teaspoon fresh thyme leaves
  or minced rosemary

4 cloves garlic, minced

1 (28-ounce) can diced tomatoes

⅓ cup kalamata olives, pitted
  and cut into quarters

20 fresh basil leaves, sliced into
  a chiffonade (see pg 19)

1. Preheat the oven to 375°. In a large bowl, toss the eggplant with 2 tablespoons of the olive oil, ½ teaspoon salt, and a few grindings of pepper; toss until evenly coated. Transfer to a baking sheet and arrange the eggplant cut side down. In the same bowl, repeat with the zucchini, 2 more tablespoons oil, ½ teaspoon salt, and some pepper, tossing and transferring to a second baking sheet.

2. Roast until the vegetables are tender and the undersides are golden brown, about 40 minutes (the eggplant and zucchini may differ in cooking time, and that is fine; remove each when cooked to perfection). Let the vegetables rest for 5 minutes on the baking sheet before removing with a thin spatula. This gives them a chance to steam themselves off the pan's surface, so you don't leave any of their sweet crust behind.

3. Meanwhile, in a large sauté pan, heat the remaining 2 tablespoons oil over medium heat. Add the onion, peppers, and thyme, and cook until the onions are translucent and the pepper softened, about 5 minutes. Add the garlic and cook 2 minutes more. Add the tomatoes and olives, and cook, partially covered, until the tomatoes break down and the mixture is thickened slightly, about 10 minutes.

4. Stir in the roasted eggplant and zucchini, and season to taste with more salt and pepper. Stir the basil in at the last minute, so it just wilts. Serve warm or at room temperature.

Roasted Cauliflower with Tomatoes and Capers

Roasting is by far the best way to prepare cauliflower, rendering it creamy and caramelized all at once. Cauliflower has a natural affinity for pairing with almost everything, and this recipe takes it to the limit, combining it with hot, sour, salty, and sweet elements all at once.

SERVES 4

1 head cauliflower, cut into 3-inch florets (the stalk is very edible)

6 tablespoons extra-virgin olive oil

Kosher salt and a pepper mill

3 cloves garlic, thinly sliced

2 anchovy fillets

¼ teaspoon crushed red pepper flakes

2 large tomatoes, roughly chopped

2 tablespoons capers

2 tablespoons currants or minced raisins

Pinch of saffron (optional)

1. Preheat the oven to 375°. In a large mixing bowl, combine the cauliflower florets with 3 tablespoons of the oil, 1 teaspoon salt, and a few grindings of pepper; toss until evenly coated. Transfer to a rimmed baking sheet and arrange all the vegetables cut side down.

2. Roast until the florets are tender and the undersides are golden brown, about 30 minutes. Let the vegetables rest for 5 minutes on the baking sheet before removing with a thin spatula. This gives them a chance to steam themselves off the pan's surface, so you don't leave any of their sweet crust behind.

3. Meanwhile, in a large sauté pan, heat the remaining 3 tablespoons of oil over medium heat. Add the garlic, anchovies, and pepper flakes, and cook until the anchovies melt, about 2 minutes. Add the tomatoes, capers, currants, and saffron (if using), and cook until the tomatoes are saucy, about 5 minutes. Add the roasted cauliflower and cook until heated through. Serve warm or at room temperature.

Chile-Roasted Broccoli with Garlic

Roasting broccoli in a very hot oven gives it a big boost of flavor. The florets have time to develop a bit of crispy char, elevating a vegetable that is traditionally blanched to new heights.

SERVES 6

1 head broccoli, cut into 4-inch florets (the stalk is very edible)

3 tablespoons extra-virgin olive oil

¼ teaspoon crushed red pepper flakes

3 cloves garlic, thinly sliced

¼ cup water

Kosher salt

1. Preheat the oven to 450°. In a large bowl, combine the broccoli, oil, pepper flakes, garlic, water, and ½ teaspoon salt and toss to coat. Transfer to a rimmed baking sheet and arrange the broccoli in a single layer.

2. Roast until the broccoli is tender and lightly charred, about 10 minutes. Serve warm or at room temperature.

String Beans with Lemon Gremolata - pg 76

Blanching Green Vegetables

Blanching is a cooking method that creates vivid and crisp-tender green vegetables by submerging them in well-salted boiling water. It is a beloved chef's technique and also has a lot of value for the home cook. Blanching cooks vegetables evenly and efficiently, either to enjoy right away or to have on hand for future meals.

Materials
Wide, deep pot with a lid
Tongs
Colander or long-handled wire strainer
(called a "spider")

Ingredients
Green vegetables
(broccoli, broccoli rabe, string beans, asparagus, snap peas, snow peas, Brussels sprouts)
Kosher salt

Preparing

FIRST, REMOVE THE TOUGH PARTS:

1 ASPARAGUS: Snap the whitish-purple base off the bottom of the stalks (1 to 3 inches — the thicker the asparagus, the more you will need to remove); it will naturally snap off where the vegetable is tender enough to eat.

2 SNAP PEAS/SNOW PEAS: Pinch off the top stem and pull away the string that runs along the straight side of the vegetable. Note: Not all of them have strings, so if you're lucky, you won't find any.

3 BROCCOLI RABE: Cut off the bottom 3 inches of the stalk; it's too stringy to enjoy.

4 BROCCOLI AND CAULIFLOWER: Cut into small florets, keeping at least 3 inches of stalk attached (it is very edible).

5 STRING BEANS: Pinch off the top stem end; leave the "tails" intact.

6 BRUSSELS SPROUTS: Trim off the browned base and any outer leaves that come away with it; cut in half lengthwise.

CHEFS SAY

Don't skimp on the salt!

The water used to blanch vegetables (and cook pasta) should taste salty, like the sea. You need 1 tablespoon of kosher salt for every 6 cups of water to make a properly salted pot of blanching water. The small amount of salted water that vegetables absorb during blanching helps bring out their sweetness; using unsalted water only dilutes their flavor. Almost all of the cooking water goes down the drain, so don't be concerned about "all that salt."

Salt + fat + acid = the flavor trifecta.

When seasoning even the simplest of foods (like blanched asparagus and string beans or lettuce leaves), remember 3 important ingredients: salt, fat, and acid. These are the building blocks of flavor and together, they make everything taste its best. Consider these combos when looking to season your vegetables: salt, butter, and lemon (we use this combo about 98% of the time); salt, extra-virgin olive oil, and red-wine vinegar; soy sauce, toasted sesame oil, and rice vinegar.

To make better broccoli rabe, please squeeze.

The secret to flavorful broccoli rabe is squeezing it dry after blanching. Water gets trapped in broccoli rabe's porous stalk and the leaves. After blanching, run the rabe under cold water until cool enough to handle. Take small handfuls of the rabe and firmly squeeze them over the sink. The less water, the more flavor. Cut the squeezed rabe in 2-inch pieces and season as you like (try our Garlicky Broccoli Rabe recipe, pg 72).

Blanching

1. Bring a large, covered pot of water to a boil.

2. Sufficiently salt the water: 1 tablespoon of kosher salt for every 6 cups of water (the water must be salty).

3. Using tongs, add the vegetables to the boiling water and submerge below the waterline.

4. Do not re-cover the pot. Acids released through steam during cooking can mar the vegetables' bright green color if they drip back into the pot.

5. Cook for 3 minutes* (the water may not return to a boil, and that is fine), then start taste-testing for crisp-tenderness, which is the ideal texture for blanched green vegetables. They should not taste raw or overcooked to limpness. Older, tougher vegetables may need up to 4 minutes.

Draining

TWO OPTIONS:

- Drain the pot into a colander set in the sink, or

- Remove the vegetables to a bowl using a pair of tongs or a wire strainer (spider).

Shocking

"Shocking" is restaurant-speak for rapidly cooling food. Since you are not cooking massive amounts of vegetables like restaurants do, your cool-down method need not involve the ice bath that lends this technique its dramatic name. You can simply run the vegetables under cold water until they are cool to the touch.

If you are eating the vegetables right away, you can skip this step. However, keep in mind that vegetables sitting in a hot heap in a colander or bowl will continue cooking, which may compromise their vibrant green color and crisp-tender texture if they're left for more than 5 minutes.

* TWO-MINUTE VEGETABLES

Some vegetables need less than 3 minutes of cooking to be perfectly crisp-tender: slim haricots verts, snap peas, snow peas, pencil-thin asparagus, and broccoli rabe (if you like its bitter bite) should all be tested for doneness at the 2-minute mark.

STUDENTS ASK

Do I need to shock my vegetables if I'm eating them right away?

No, though it can't hurt. If you are truly ready to sit down to your meal, then tossing the vegetables with a salt-fat-acid combo and serving them straight away is perfectly fine. But don't leave them sitting in a hot heap for longer than 5 minutes or they will indeed move beyond their ideal texture.

Do vegetables lose their vitamins when you blanch them?

Yes, there is always some loss of vitamins when you subject vegetables to any cooking process, so it is important to seek vitamins from raw fruits and vegetables too. But keep in mind that the fibrous roughage (dietary fiber) and minerals (like calcium and iron) in cooked greens are still very good reasons to eat a lot of them. They fill you up and support good digestion like nothing other than a plant can.

Is blanching vegetables better than steaming?

Yes, we think so. Steaming takes longer and does not produce as evenly cooked vegetables as plunging them into boiling water. But we recognize that people love to steam vegetables (it sounds so gentle and lovely!), so feel free to use your steamer basket to cook your green vegetables, if you prefer. The vegetables will take a bit longer to cook but you can prep, shock, and season them the same way as blanched vegetables.

Snappy Peas with Orange-Sesame Butter

This orange-sesame butter is addictive and a great seasoning for most blanched green vegetables, particularly snap peas, asparagus, broccoli, string beans, and snow peas.

SERVES 4

Kosher salt

1 pound snap peas or snow peas, strings removed (see Preparing, pg 66)

2 tablespoons unsalted butter

3 tablespoons sesame seeds

Grated zest of ½ orange

1 tablespoon toasted sesame oil

1 teaspoon fresh lemon juice or rice vinegar

1. Bring a large pot of salty water (1 tablespoon salt per 6 cups water) to a boil over high heat. Add the snap peas to the boiling water and submerge below the waterline. Cook until bright green and crisp-tender, testing for doneness after 2 minutes. Remove with a wire strainer or drain into a colander set in the sink. Run under cold water until they are cool to the touch.

2. In a large sauté pan, heat the butter over medium heat. Add the sesame seeds and orange zest, and cook until the seeds just start to turn golden, about 2 minutes. Add the snap peas and sesame oil and cook until warmed through. Remove from heat and add the lemon juice, and season with a generous pinch of salt. Serve warm or at room temperature.

Garlicky Broccoli Rabe

This is how you make delicious broccoli rabe. Along with squeezing the water out of the cooked rabe to concentrate its flavor, the other trick is to season it with plenty of garlic, hot pepper flakes, and salty Parmigiano-Reggiano cheese. To make this dish a full meal, add a can of drained (but not rinsed) chickpeas when you add the chopped rabe to the pan in step 3, and serve over cooked pasta or polenta.

SERVES 4

Kosher salt

1 bunch broccoli rabe, bottom 3 inches of stalk discarded (see Preparing, pg 66)

¼ cup extra-virgin olive oil

3 cloves garlic, minced

¼ teaspoon crushed red pepper flakes

2 tablespoons chicken broth or water

Parmigiano-Reggiano cheese, for serving

1. Bring a large pot of salty water (1 tablespoon salt per 6 cups water) to a boil over high heat. Using tongs, add the broccoli rabe to the boiling water and submerge below the waterline. Cook until bright green and crisp-tender, testing for doneness after 2 minutes. Remove with tongs or drain into a colander set in the sink. Run under cold water until they are cool to the touch to stop them from cooking and set their vivid color.

2. Take 3 blanched stalks and firmly squeeze them over the sink to remove as much water from the stalks and leaves as you can. Repeat with the rest of the rabe. Cut the stalks into 2-inch pieces and set aside.

3. In a large sauté pan set over medium heat, combine the oil, garlic, and pepper flakes. When the garlic becomes fragrant, about 2 minutes, add the chopped broccoli rabe and broth, and cook until the rabe is warmed through. Remove from heat and season with salt and a generous grating of Parmigiano-Reggiano cheese. Serve warm or at room temperature.

Asparagus with Orange–Smoked Paprika Vinaigrette

Smoked paprika and orange zest add new dimension to a traditional vinaigrette. These flavors would also be welcome on blanched string beans, snap peas, and broccoli.

SERVES 4

Kosher salt and a pepper mill

1 bunch asparagus, tough ends discarded (see Preparing, pg 66)

1 small shallot, diced small

Grated zest and juice of ½ navel or blood orange

1 teaspoon smoked paprika

1 tablespoon sherry vinegar or red wine vinegar

3 tablespoons extra-virgin olive oil, or more to taste

1 large navel, blood, or Cara Cara orange, peeled and cut into thin rounds

1. Bring a large pot of salty water (1 tablespoon salt per 6 cups water) to a boil over high heat. Using tongs, add the asparagus to the boiling water and submerge below the waterline. Cook until bright green and crisp-tender, testing for doneness after 3 minutes. Remove with tongs or drain into a colander set in the sink. Run under cold water until they are cool to the touch to stop them from cooking and set their vivid color. Arrange on a serving platter.

2. Meanwhile, in a small glass jar with a lid, combine the shallot, orange zest and juice, paprika, vinegar, and a good pinch of salt. Let stand for 15 minutes to allow the flavors to develop.

3. Add the olive oil into the vinegar mixture and shake vigorously until completely blended. Season with a few grindings of pepper and a bit more salt, if necessary (dip a blanched asparagus spear in the dressing to taste it — a better way to judge than with your finger). Pour the vinaigrette over the asparagus and garnish with the orange rounds. Serve warm or at room temperature.

Broccoli with Toasted Almonds

This recipe is based on the classic French "amandine" (with almonds) preparation, which seasons vegetables with golden-brown almonds, butter, and lemon juice. This flavor trio is also a winner with blanched string beans, asparagus, and Brussels sprouts.

SERVES 4

Kosher salt

1 bunch broccoli, cut into 4-inch florets (the stalk is very edible)

2 tablespoons unsalted butter

1 tablespoon extra-virgin olive oil

¼ cup slivered or sliced almonds

1 small shallot, sliced thin

Juice of ½ lemon

1. Bring a large pot of salty water (1 tablespoon salt per 6 cups water) to a boil over high heat. Using tongs, add the broccoli to the boiling water and submerge below the waterline. Cook until bright green and crisp-tender, testing for doneness after 3 minutes. Remove with tongs or drain into a colander set in the sink. Run under cold water until they are cool to the touch.

2. In a large sauté pan, heat the butter and oil over medium heat. When the butter is melted and bubbling, add the almonds and shallot and cook, stirring frequently, until the nuts start to turn golden, about 3 minutes. Add the broccoli and cook, tossing, until warmed through. Remove from heat, add the lemon juice, and season with a generous pinch of salt. Serve warm or at room temperature.

Brussels Sprouts with Bacon, Red Onion, and Pecans

Brussels sprouts need a rich fat to soften their bitter flavor. Bacon is a natural choice, but butter can also be used. Sweet red onions and nutty pecans further tame the sprouts.

SERVES 4

Kosher salt and a pepper mill

1 pound Brussels sprouts, root ends trimmed, cut in half lengthwise

3 slices thick-cut bacon, cut crosswise into ¼-inch pieces

1 small red onion, diced

⅓ cup chopped pecans

2 teaspoons Dijon mustard

1 tablespoon red wine vinegar or apple cider vinegar

1. Bring a large pot of salty water (1 tablespoon salt per 6 cups water) to a boil over high heat. Using tongs, add the sprouts to the boiling water and submerge below the water line. Cook until bright green and crisp-tender, testing for doneness after 3 minutes. Remove with tongs or drain into a colander set in the sink. Run under cold water until they are cool to the touch.

2. In a large sauté pan over medium heat, cook the bacon until it is crisp and has rendered its fat, about 8 minutes. Using a slotted spoon, transfer the bacon to a paper towel to drain. When cool, crumble the bacon and set aside.

3. To the hot fat in the pan, add the onion and cook until golden, about 6 minutes. Add the Brussels sprouts and pecans and cook, stirring often, until the sprouts are golden brown in spots and heated through, about 5 minutes. Stir in the mustard and vinegar, and season with a generous pinch of salt and a few grindings of pepper. Sprinkle with the bacon and serve warm.

String Beans with Lemon Gremolata

Gremolata is a bright herbal sprinkle made from fresh parsley, garlic, and citrus zest. Traditionally used atop long-cooked meat dishes to cut their richness, it is also a terrific way to perk up any blanched or roasted vegetables. You can substitute minced dill or cilantro for some of the parsley to vary the flavor. Gremolata is best used on vegetables served warm or at room temperature.

SERVES 4

Kosher salt

¼ cup minced flat-leaf parsley

1 large clove garlic, minced fine

Grated zest and juice of 1 lemon

1 pound string beans, tops removed, tails intact

3 tablespoons extra-virgin olive oil

1. Bring a large pot of salty water (1 tablespoon salt per 6 cups water) to a boil over high heat. Meanwhile, in a small bowl, combine the parsley, garlic, and zest, and set aside.

2. Using tongs, add the string beans to the boiling water and submerge below the waterline. Cook until bright green and crisp-tender, testing for doneness after 3 minutes. Remove with tongs or drain into a colander set in the sink. Run under cold water until they are cool to the touch to stop them from cooking and set their vivid color. Arrange on a serving platter.

3. Drizzle the string beans with the olive oil and 2 tablespoons lemon juice. Sprinkle the gremolata mixture over the top and finish with a dusting of salt. Serve at room temperature.

Swiss Chard with Garlic and Lemon - pg 84

Cooking Leafy Greens

Leafy greens are your ticket to a long, healthy life. It is vital to know how to prepare them well, so you can eat a lot of them. The goal of this chapter is to turn you into the kind of cook who gazes in happy anticipation at the piles of bunched greens at the market. Listen to your mother: "Eat your greens."

Materials

12-inch stainless-steel sauté pan with a lid
Wooden spoon
Large mixing bowl
(for washing leaves)

Ingredients

Leafy greens
(spinach, arugula, Swiss chard, mustard greens, escarole, bok choy, kale, collard greens)
Kosher salt

COLLARD GREENS

MUSTARD GREENS

LACINATO KALE

SWISS CHARD

Removing the Stalks

For leafy greens with a tough inner stalk (like kale, collard greens, mustard greens, and Swiss chard), you need to remove the stalks before shredding the leaves. In most cases, you will discard the stalks. Remove with the tip of a knife, cutting along the stalk to where it narrows to about ½ inch thick, or strip it out with your hands. To do this, loosen a bit of the leaf from both sides of the stalk at the bottom of the leaf. Grab hold of the stalk with one hand and gently pull the frayed leaf upward with the other, stripping it away from the stalk.

CHEFS SAY

Save your chard stalks!

We like to thinly slice the brightly colored stalks of Swiss chard and cook them with the leaves for texture. Since they take longer to soften than the leaves, add the sliced stalks to the hot, oiled pan for 3 minutes on their own before adding garlic or greens to the pan, so they can get a head start on tenderness.

Boldly season your greens.

Try these flavorful ingredient combinations:

To the hot oil, add one or more of the following and cook for 2 minutes before adding greens: crushed red pepper flakes, anchovy fillets (they will dissolve when cooked), finely minced ginger, minced garlic, or chopped nuts or seeds (sliced almonds, pumpkin seeds).

When adding the greens, include one or more: chopped raisins, dried currants, sliced olives, capers, or sliced cherry tomatoes. Always season with salt and an acid before serving to bring the most flavor out of the greens and add-ins.

Think greens for dinner.

Most menu planning centers a meal around a piece of meat. Consider turning that on its head and making leafy greens your meal's focal point. All the recipes in this chapter can be made into a full meal by adding a protein (chicken, shrimp, chickpeas, cannellini beans) to the greens during cooking, and serving alongside a cooked grain (rice, polenta, farro, quinoa, pasta, or even a hunk of crusty bread).

Washing the Leaves

Leafy greens can be gritty and dirty, especially if they are from the farmers market. Even those bunches from the supermarket need a good cleaning. Don't be tempted to simply pass the leaves under running water; that rarely does a good job of removing hidden dirt.

TO PROPERLY WASH LEAFY GREENS:

1. Fill your largest bowl with water and submerge the leaves, giving them a good swish around so the water gets into all the nooks and crannies (especially important for ridged leaves like kale, chard, and curly spinach, which hide dirt well).

2. Lift the leaves out of the bowl and transfer to a colander. If there is any grit left over in the bottom of the bowl, empty it and repeat until the water is clear.

1. Lay whole, de-stalked leaves on top of each other.

Shredding the Leaves

Larger leaves, like Swiss chard, kale, and collards, must be cut down to size to make them manageable to cook and eat. Greens shrink considerably when cooked, so they need only be sliced into wide strips before cooking. Smaller and more tender leaves, like spinach and arugula, can be cooked whole.

2. Roll crosswise into a tight cylinder.

3. Slice crosswise into 1-inch strips.

LEAFY GREEN TENDERNESS SCALE
The tenderness/toughness of a leaf determines its approximate cooking time. Here are guidelines for 1 bunch; larger quantities will increase cooking time by a few minutes:

Spinach, arugula – **2 minutes**

Escarole, bok choy – **4 minutes**

Mustard greens – **5 minutes**

Swiss chard – **5 minutes**

Kale – **6 minutes**

Collards – **12 minutes, or more**

Cooking the Leaves

1. Heat enough fat (butter or extra-virgin olive oil) to coat the bottom of your pan, at least 2 tablespoons. Add the minced garlic (and pepper flakes, if desired) and cook for 1 minute, allowing the garlic's pungent oils to transfer to the fat, where it can properly coat and season every crevice of your greens. Don't let it brown, which will mar its flavor.

2. Add the greens and cook, stirring constantly, until wilted and tender. This can take 2 to 12 minutes, depending on the tenderness of your greens. If cooking a large amount of greens, cover with a lid for the first 2 minutes to help them wilt down more quickly. Remove the lid and continue cooking, uncovered, until tender.

3. Tough leafy greens, like kale and collards, benefit from a longer cooking time to properly soften. To move things along, add a splash of liquid (broth or water; about ¼ cup to start) to the greens while cooking to help steam them and prevent them from drying out during the prolonged cooking time.

4. Just before serving, season your greens with salt and an acid (1 tablespoon lemon juice or 1 teaspoon of red wine vinegar or cider vinegar to start). Then taste, repeat as needed, and taste again until the greens are full of flavor (salt) and brightness (acid).

Tuscan Kale with Almonds and Raisins

Raisins or dried currants are a terrific addition to any cooked leafy green. Their burst of sweetness is exactly what earthy greens need. We recommend lacinato kale (see photo, pg 80), the most tender of the kale varieties, which also goes by a few other names: cavolo nero, Tuscan, and dinosaur. It has a green-black color and a bumpy surface. This recipe is also delicious with Swiss chard. Adding a can of drained cannellini beans will turn this pan of greens into a meal.

SERVES 4

3 tablespoons extra-virgin olive oil

3 tablespoons sliced or slivered almonds

2 cloves garlic, minced

2 anchovy fillets in oil (optional but delicious) or 1 tablespoon capers

1 large bunch kale, tough center stalks removed (see Removing the Stalks, pg 80), washed and cut into 1-inch chiffonade (see pg 19)

2 tablespoons dried currants or minced raisins

Kosher salt and a pepper mill

Juice of ½ lemon

In a large sauté pan, heat the oil over medium heat. Add the almonds and cook until they just start to color, about 3 minutes. Add the garlic and anchovies and cook until fragrant and the anchovies have melted, about 2 minutes more. Add the kale and currants and cook, tossing with tongs, until the leaves are wilted, about 6 minutes. Season with a generous pinch of salt and a few grindings of pepper. Finish with the lemon juice and serve warm.

Swiss Chard Puttanesca

Puttanesca is an extra-flavorful, tomato-based pasta sauce, packed with salty, briny, and pungent ingredients. These same flavors also work wonders with a hearty bunch of chard. To turn this recipe into a full meal, stir in 1 (14-ounce) can of drained, but not rinsed, chickpeas toward the end of cooking and serve over your favorite pasta shape.

SERVES 4

1 large bunch chard, tough center stalks removed and reserved (see Removing the Stalks, pg 80), washed and cut into 1-inch chiffonade (see pg 19)

2 tablespoons extra-virgin olive oil

½ small onion, diced

3 cloves garlic, minced

2 whole anchovy fillets

¼ teaspoon crushed red pepper flakes

2 medium tomatoes, diced, or 1 cup halved cherry tomatoes

2 tablespoons capers

¼ cup chopped kalamata olives

Kosher salt

1. Thinly slice the chard stalks and set aside.

2. In a large sauté pan, heat the oil over medium heat. Add the onion and sliced stalks and cook until softened, about 3 minutes. Add the garlic, anchovies, and pepper flakes and cook until the anchovies dissolve, about 1 minute. Add the tomatoes and cook until they become saucy, about 3 minutes. Add the chard, capers, and olives, and cook until the leaves have wilted and are tender, stirring constantly, about 5 minutes. Season to taste with salt, if needed (the capers, olives, and anchovies are already quite salty), and serve warm or at room temperature.

Gingery Bok Choy with Tomatoes and Sesame

This is a deeply satisfying, somewhat soupy pot of Asian greens. Bok choy has a pleasant mustard bite to it and plays well with tomatoes, sesame, and ginger. Adding uncooked shrimp to the pan when you add the tomatoes and bok choy will afford you a delicious, full meal when served over rice or Asian noodles.

SERVES 4

2 tablespoons extra-virgin olive oil or
   a neutral oil (see pg 31)

1 tablespoon finely minced ginger

3 cloves garlic, minced

3 plum tomatoes, cut into thin slices,
   or 1 cup cherry tomatoes, cut in half

1 pound baby bok choy, washed and
   cut into 2-inch pieces

2 tablespoons soy sauce

2 tablespoons chicken broth

2 tablespoons toasted sesame oil

1 tablespoon rice vinegar or
   white wine vinegar

Kosher salt

Sriracha hot sauce, for serving
   (optional)

In a large sauté pan, heat the oil over medium heat. Add the ginger and garlic and cook until fragrant, about 1 minute. Add the tomatoes and bok choy and cook until the vegetables start to wilt, stirring constantly, about 4 minutes. Add the soy sauce, broth, sesame oil, and vinegar and cook for 1 minute. Season with a pinch of salt. Serve warm with hot sauce, if desired.

Escarole with Cannellini Beans

Escarole is a soft leafy green used in Italian cooking. It has a pleasing bitter edge like many of Italy's beloved greens (broccoli rabe, radicchio, arugula). This side dish is easily transformed into a fantastic, dinner-worthy soup by adding 4 cups of chicken broth in place of the lemon juice or balsamic vinegar, cooking for 10 additional minutes (to really soften the leaves), and serving with a generous grating of Parmigiano-Reggiano cheese and some crusty bread.

SERVES 4

¼ cup extra-virgin olive oil

4 cloves garlic, minced or sliced

¼ teaspoon crushed red pepper flakes

1 large head escarole, washed and
   cut into 1-inch pieces (the whole leaf
   is edible)

Kosher salt

1 (14-ounce) can cannellini beans,
   drained

Juice of ½ lemon, or 1 tablespoon
   balsamic vinegar, as needed

In a large sauté pan, heat the olive oil over medium heat. Add the garlic and pepper flakes and cook for 1 minute. Add the escarole and ½ teaspoon salt and cook, stirring, until the escarole is wilted and tender, about 4 minutes. Stir in the beans and cook until heated through. Season with more salt, if needed. Finish with 1 tablespoon lemon juice to start (or balsamic if you want a sweeter dish), adding more as needed until the flavors are bright. Serve warm.

Creamy Lemon Spinach

Creamed spinach cannot be beat. The addition of ample lemon zest and lemon juice sets this recipe apart from the rest, making it light, bright, and deeply satisfying. You can also substitute 1 large bunch of Swiss chard for the spinach; before cooking, remove the stalks and slice the leaves into ½-inch-wide strips (see pg 83).

SERVES 4

2 tablespoons extra-virgin olive oil

1 small onion, diced

2 teaspoons all-purpose flour

2 large bunches fresh spinach,
  stems removed, washed, or
    10 ounces baby spinach

½ cup heavy cream

Grated zest and juice of 1 lemon

Kosher salt and a pepper mill

1. In a large sauté pan, heat the oil over medium heat. Add the onion and cook until very soft and golden, about 5 minutes. Sprinkle the flour over the onions and cook for 1 minute. Add the spinach, in batches if necessary, and cook, uncovered, until just wilted, about 3 minutes.

2. Stir in the cream, lemon zest, ½ teaspoon salt, and a few grindings of pepper. Cook until the mixture thickens a bit, about 2 minutes. Add 2 tablespoons of lemon juice to start and then taste, seasoning with more salt and lemon juice as needed. Serve warm.

Braised Collard Greens with Bacon and Onions

Braising, a cooking method that uses flavorful liquid to cook food, offers just the right environment for softening tough collard greens into sublimeness. Bacon lends its smoky-salty goodness to this velvety pot of greens.

SERVES 4

3 strips bacon, cut into ½-inch pieces

1 large onion, sliced

2 cloves garlic, minced

¼ teaspoon crushed red pepper flakes

1 pound collard greens (or any leafy green: Swiss chard, mustard greens, turnip greens, kale), tough center stalks removed (see Removing the Stalks, pg 80), washed and cut into 1-inch chiffonade (see pg 19)

½ cup chicken broth

1 tablespoon red wine vinegar or apple cider vinegar

Kosher salt

1. In a large sauté pan with a lid, heat the bacon over medium heat. Cook until it is crisp and has rendered its fat, about 8 minutes. Add the onions and cook in the bacon fat until very soft and just beginning to brown, about 6 minutes. Add the garlic and pepper flakes and cook for 1 minute more.

2. Add the collard greens, broth, vinegar, and ½ teaspoon salt to the pan and bring the broth to a boil. Cover, reduce heat to medium-low, and cook the collards until they are very tender, at least 12 minutes. Season generously with more salt and vinegar as needed to brighten the flavors. Serve warm.

Recommended Kitchen Equipment

Having the right equipment really makes a difference in the kitchen. Use this list as a guide for building your collection.

Basic Pots & Pans

This should be heavy-duty, stainless-steel cookware with metal (read: ovenproof) handles. Do not invest in a whole set of nonstick cookware; it is only necessary to have 1 skillet with a nonstick coating.

❶ 1½- and 3-quart saucepans with covers

❷ 6- to 8-quart Dutch oven or saucepot with cover (depending on your family size or entertaining aspirations)

❸ 8-quart stockpot (for blanching vegetables/cooking pasta)

Basic Pots & Pans
Continued...

1. 12-inch sauté pan (sloped sides) or skillet (straight sides) with cover (2)
2. 12-inch nonstick sauté pan
3. 10-inch sauté pan

Measuring Tools

1. Set of dry measuring cups
2. Set of measuring spoons
3. 2-cup liquid measuring cup
4. Kitchen timer
5. Instant-read meat thermometer

Preparation Tools

❶ Large utensil holder, to place near stove

❷ Stainless-steel tongs (with locking mechanism) (2)

❸ Wooden spoons (1 with a flat-edged tip) (3)

❹ Flexible rubber spatula

❺ Large solid metal spoon (2)

❻ Ladle

❼ Stainless-steel spatula ("pancake turner")

❽ Kitchen shears

❾ Lemon/lime juicer

❿ Potato masher

⓫ Microplane grater

⓬ Vegetable peeler

⓭ Pastry brush

⓮ Large wire whisk

⓯ Can opener

Preparation Equipment

❶ Pepper mill (Peugeot brand offers the best grinding mechanism, ranging from coarse to fine; check the bottom of the grinder for the name)

❷ Wooden or soft plastic cutting boards (2)

❸ 9 x 9- and 9 x 13-inch baking dishes (heatproof glass or ceramic)

❹ Heavy-gauge baking sheets (also called half sheet pans) (2)

❺ Reusable nonstick baking mat (never grease a cookie sheet again!) (2)

❻ Kitchen towels (at least 6)

❼ Pot holders or oven mitts (2)

❽ Stainless-steel mixing bowls, graduated sizes

❾ Colander

❿ Box grater

⓫ Salad spinner

High-Carbon-Steel Knives

Wusthof, Henckels, and Mundial provide excellent quality.

❶ 8-inch chef's knife

❷ 8-inch serrated knife

❸ Handheld 2-stage knife sharpener

❹ 3½-inch paring knife

Appliances

Resist the temptation to buy too many appliances for the kitchen. Most, with the following exceptions, don't often save you time or hassle, and take up more room than they are worth.

❶ Food processor (11 cup or larger)

❷ Hand-held or standing electric mixer

❸ Blender

Jennifer Clair

Jennifer Clair is a culinary instructor and the founder of Home Cooking New York, a cooking school in downtown New York City. Before launching the school in 2002, she honed her culinary and editorial chops as a Food Editor at *Martha Stewart Living* and the Recipes Editor at *The Wall Street Journal*. She graduated from the Institute of Culinary Education on a full James Beard Foundation scholarship. Jennifer's first cookbook is *Gourmet Cooking on a Budget* (2010). She lives in the Hudson Valley, NY, with her husband and two children.

The Story of Home Cooking New York

Home Cooking New York began in 2002 as a mobile business that offered cooking classes in students' home kitchens across New York City. In 2008, we branched out into public cooking classes upon discovering a fully stocked kitchen for rent in the back of a local bed and breakfast. After moving and growing several more times, we finally built out our own welcoming teaching kitchen in a former textile factory in downtown Manhattan. Home Cooking New York is now a 7-days-a-week cooking school, with a rotating crew of many marvelous chef-instructors. Please pay us a visit the next time you're in town.

To learn more about Home Cooking New York (and receive free weekly recipes), please visit the school online at www.homecookingny.com.

Acknowledgments

Now is my chance to gush about all the good people who have made Home Cooking New York a success and were instrumental in bringing this cookbook to fruition.

Chef John Scoff became my first official employee back in 2004, turning my one-woman enterprise into a real business. He was, and still is, just the kind of fellow you want to spend time with in your kitchen. An impressive culinary pedigree alone does not make a successful chef-instructor (although that is required); it is who you are as a person. John's generosity as a human being set the benchmark for all the instructors who would come after him.

Chef Erica Wides joined us in 2014, right after we built out our new kitchen and could finally offer classes 7 days a week. She is smart and sassy and brings a vivaciousness and hilarity to every class she teaches. With 15 years of experience teaching professional culinary students before making her way to us, she is a powerhouse of food knowledge, and was the culinary editor for this book.

Susana Tinizhanay completes the "dream team" that makes up the core of our school. She keeps the school in order and sparkly clean and is the thread that ties us all together. Anyone who runs a kitchen will tell you that your cleaning staff is your greatest asset. Susana is the perfect example; in fact, she breaks the mold. I am grateful for her at least twice a day.

This book — the culmination of my two great pleasures, food and writing — was finally pushed into the world with the help of many friends who are also at the top of their professional game. Julie Bickar helped me find my voice (which was harder to access than I thought) when I first began writing, and also uncovered the voice of our students which you will find throughout the book. Julie Shiroishi was my first official "reader," and gave me the thumbs up I needed to press on.

Meredith Heuer, a good friend and culinary collaborator for years, is also a top-notch food and lifestyle photographer for the likes of *The New York Times* and the former *Gourmet*. The chance to actually work together at her bright photo studio in Newburgh, NY, was so thrilling that I kept coming up with reshoot ideas just so we could keep laughing and bickering together as we created the lovely photographs for this book.

Choosing the designer for this book was a no-brainer. Dan Weise has branded a large swath of the local businesses in our town of Beacon, NY, and has both the perfect eye and keen food interest needed to combine Meredith's photography and my instructions into a brilliantly readable and beautifully composed book.

I am surrounded by a family that relishes the intricacies of the English language, which comes in quite handy when you need willing and able people to read a book you are writing. My sister, Kate Herman, is an exacting copy editor and vocabulary maven. My brother, Jon Herman, is a craftsman with words and a novice cook who asked all the right questions. My husband, Stephen Clair, wielded his magic editing pen and slashed my prose to pieces, until it was clean and shiny. He is merciless, and masterful.

Our children, Esther and Henry, were more engaged in this cookbook than I could have dared to hope. They chimed in — with conviction! — about it all: the photography, my wardrobe for photo shoots, and the deliciousness (or not) of various recipe tests. Their love and appreciation of food creates a soul-deep satisfaction in me.

The two people I am most grateful for, my parents, Phyllis and Ivan Herman, are no longer here to cheer me on. But they always did, from my earliest memories, and they are the reason I am filled with the can-do spirit. They were both excellent wordsmiths and deeply loving parents. This book would have made them kvell with joy.

Index

Page numbers in *italics* indicate recipe photos.

2.
   s
   sa
   ara
   and
3. Slic

BLAN
FOR G
VEG
SHOCK
or, NO SALT
ACID — FA
   ↓
   CITRUS
   VINEGARS
   WINE

© Home Cooking New Yo
www.homecookingny.com

Seared Steak with Red Wine–Shallot Sauce
Serves 4

2 (about 1 1/2 pounds) hanger, rib-eye, or strip steaks
Coarse salt and freshly ground black pepper
tablespoons extra virgin olive oil
edium shallots, thinly sliced
p good red wine
p good-quality chicken broth
sprig fresh thyme
poon unsalted butter

e steaks and season with salt and pepper. Heat a cast-iron or heavy skillet over
gh heat until very hot. Add 1 tablespoon of the oil and when it begins to smoke, add
Cook them until they are well browned on both sides and until they register 125° on
ad thermometer for medium-rare, about 4 minutes per side. (Take the temperature of
serting the thermometer into the side of the steak, so you get a more accurate
at from the top, which is not deep enough.) Transfer the steaks to a cutting board
st for 5 minutes.
ke the pan sauce: Add the remaining tablespoon of oil to the hot skillet. Cook the
and lightly browned, about 5 minutes. Add the wine, broth, and thyme sprig
sauce is reduced by half, about 6 minutes. Remove the skillet from the heat
ter. Remove the thyme sprig and season with salt and pepper.
½-inch-thick pieces and serve drizzled with the warm sauce.

Handwritten notes:

STEAK → VERY HOT PAN
MEAT DROPS PAN TEMP
DRY MEAT

SEASON SIDE DOWN
DON'T MOVE IT

120 RARE
DON'T USE THERMOMETER
125-130° MED RARE
[1 INCH] MORE THAN 1 INCH OVEN
1 INCH OVEN NEEDS

DEGLAZING
THE FOND
REDUCE 50%
WILL BOTHER
STUCK TO BE GLOSSY

RY
SHIT.

: oven finish

leavy skillet over
1 it begins to smoke, add
ntil they register 125° on
le. (Take the temperature of
ou get a more accurate
he steaks to a cutting board

oil to the hot skillet. Cook the
vine, broth, and thyme sprig
love the skillet from the heat
salt and pepper.
the warm sauce.

GLOSSY COOKED IN OIL
KNE DOWN MOST SURFACE AREA
OOKING
AS MUCH ACID

"LIKE VEGETABLES"
ROOT/HARD VEG ROAST TOGETHER
SOFT VEG ROAST TOGETHER
ROAST WITH FAT AND SALT

WHET STONE VS SHARPENER

CHEF'S KN

1 carrots